A Concise History of England

Seen Through the Eyes of a Poet

John William Skepper

A.H. STOCKWELL
PUBLISHERS SINCE 1898

Published in 2025 by
John William Skepper
in association with
Arthur H. Stockwell
West Wing Studios
Unit 166, The Mall
Luton, Bedfordshire
ahstockwell.co.uk

To my late wife, Maureen – a gracious lady and an adoring wife to me for sixty-five years.

Contents

Author's Note

I retired from a most enjoyable career in teaching in 1994 which culminated in the headship of Wheatley Hills Middle School, Doncaster. This is my second book of poems. My first anthology of poems was on a variety of topics, some humorous, some serious under the title Are You sure You Don't Like Reading Poetry? This anthology, composed in my 94th year, is based upon a study of English history, and I have attempted to set it out chronologically.

I hope readers will be able to read this as they would a factual book as the verses contain information, some of which may have been forgotten and some which may even introduce new episodes in history.

Students of history may find this a useful basis for future study.

I only wish I had had this selection of historical data available to me when I was a student.

John William Skepper

Introduction

In attempting to write the history of England in poetic form
Let me leave the reader in no doubt.
I found no problem in deciding what to include
But I had to assess carefully what to leave out.

History taught in schools from various sources
Often tended to include information not always historically checked.
So, any verse which has an exclamation or a question mark
Is inviting you to decide whether you regard it as correct.

We English are a mixture of many different races
And it's wise to check one's ancestry to verify one's identity.
The internet would help you to check your family tree.
Census returns and church records add to this amenity.

Often at school students were taught history from textbooks
And historical information tended to be accepted at face value.
Teachers should not be criticised for this as time allotted
For history lessons was often short. Perhaps this happened to you!

This anthology is designed for readers of all ages
And allows you to revisit history in a more leisurely fashion
To decide whether some historical 'facts' are true or false
And distinguish verifiable fact from fiction.

Before the development of the printing press
Some historical information was passed on verbally to the nation
And who amongst us when telling a tale
Has not enlightened it by a little exaggeration?

1: Early Invasions

My second book of poems attempts
To retell England's historic past
So I'll start by mentioning early invasion forces
Of which the Norman Conquest was the last.

The first migrants came to our shores
Probably 500,000 years ago and this was the earliest stage
Of overseas invasion with the invaders seeking land on which to settle.
Their implements were such that we refer to this period
as the Old Stone Age.

During this period the country was attached to Europe by a land bridge
So further immigration followed
from others seeking land on which to make their home.
As time passed the New Stone Age saw the development
Whereby these immigrants became settlers
rather than hunters inclined to roam.

Approximately 4,500 years ago Stonehenge was created
And the origin of the large Sarsen stones has been a mystery.
But chemical analysis has proved they came from West Woods,
Only 8 miles from Stonehenge. So, we can update our history.

Stonehenge was assembled over numerous years on Salisbury Plain
And there are many theories
on how these very heavy bluestones were brought.
The use of tree-trunk rollers is the most acceptable of these.
Perhaps, dear reader, you could provide other solutions
by giving it some thought!

When the Celts sought refuge as farmers in this country
They had two-wheel chariots
and arriving in isolated groups they soon called Britain home.
The Romans' first attempt to invade in 55BC was thwarted
but they were successful in 54 BC.
The Britons obtained peace
in return for a regular tribute to be paid to Rome.

No history would ever be complete
Without acknowledging the Romans' stay
If only to record that they built straight roads
Such as Ermine Street, Watling Street and Fosse Way.

The Celtic tribe known as the Iceni, came peacefully to settle
But the Romans took up arms against Queen Boudicca, now a widow.
She challenged them in her chariot which had knife blades on the axles
But after early success she accepted defeat which was a serious blow.

It was 43 AD before Roman rule was finally established in Britain.
They mined for lead and silver. Ironworks were started.
Eboracum, known today as York, became the military capital
And peace had finally been secured
when the Romans suddenly departed.

In AD 122 to 30 Roman Emperor Hadrian
Stopped the Picts' repeated attacks once and for all.
Between Wallsend-on-Tyne and Bowness-on-Solway
He built a ten-feet-thick defensive wall.

We owe a great deal to the Romans who provided for our defence
But their departure left us inevitably defenceless
As we had relied on the Roman Army to protect us from aggression.
During the next six-and-a-half centuries
invasions accelerated instead of getting less.

In 410 AD after three hundred years of Roman rule,
The Romans returned to their own homeland.
The Angles and Saxons gradually resumed control
With the former providing the name of 'England'.

England may owe its name to the Angles, originally Angle-Land,
But the Angles, Saxons and Jutes shared a common culture
So we usually refer to Anglo-Saxon in our ancestry
Which was significant as a milestone in our historical future.

Once the Saxons to Christianity had been converted
It was the government by priest-craft rather than brutality.
Even though such mental power may still have been abused
It was still preferable to force by physicality.

Yet England still suffered from merciless Viking invaders
Coming from Denmark and Scandinavia
Over a period of almost six generations
Until religion, language and intermarriage changed their behaviour.

The Viking King Canute tried
To stem the tidal sea, we learn!
But is it a true fact that
Saxon King Alfred some cakes did burn?

Alfred's capture of London gained acceptance as the Anglo-Saxons' leader
After he had numerous skirmishes with the Danes
And with the Danelaw many Danish words and customs
Provided our place names which today still appertains.

'By' and 'Thorpe' refer to villages or towns
And 'Toft' is the name for a homestead, so they tell me,
While 'holm' is the Danish name for an islet
And it is due to the Danes Yorkshire Ridings are only composed of three.

Of all the English monarchs,
So history books relate,
Saxon King Alfred
Was the only one judged 'Great'.

The legend of 'King Arthur', was it true or false?
Did it perhaps serve as a name for numerous knights?
Could Arthur be in Wales one moment and in Northern England the next
And be warlike against both Angles and Saxons in numerous fights?

The final successful invasion of our island shores
Was by William the Conqueror's Hastings invasion
And as no other foe has since successfully invaded
The succeeding years saw the real development of the English nation.

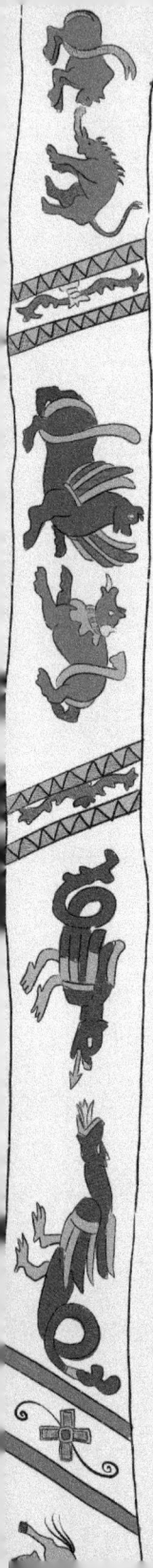

HIC AT BERGHEHÀSTEDA NOBILES LONDIN CEDVNT

2: The Middle Ages

Traditions founded in the years following the Norman Conquest,
Known as the Middle Ages or the Plantagenet generations
Are still admired by us today
And envied by less democratic nations.

Our unwritten constitution, the House of Commons,
Supremacy on the seas and our ancient universities are stories
Of success. They deserve our pride and are the basis
Of the country's freedom, prosperity and past glories.

The Feudal System enabled William to guard against future rebellions
As all land now belonged to the King who reigns.
He leased it to barons in return for fees and military service.
They allocated land to knights and knights did likewise to villeins.

The Bayeux Tapestry shows a Saxon with an arrow in his eye
But all the Saxons have armour of the same type!
King Harold Hardrada is supposed to have been shot with an arrow
Yet some textbooks suggest the arrow pierced his windpipe!

Do you accept one of those theories of Harold's death
Or could he have fallen to a Norman sword?
It is for you to decide, dear reader,
Rather than simply accepting someone else's word.

In 1086 William decided to conduct a survey of his kingdom
Which became known as the Domesday Book
because of its extensive search.
The survey included ownership of land and their dwellings,
The animals and equipment they owned
and the tithes owed to the church.

William Rufus succeeded on William II's death
But there was suspicion concerning the manner in which he dies
Ever suspecting Henry, William's brother, could have been involved.
So, dear reader, you decide for yourself on his demise!

Roger, Bishop of Salisbury, became Henry I's financial advisor.
He used a chequered cloth the finances to convey.
The department became known as the Exchequer,
A title for the Chancellor still used today.

Henry II and his descendants were often known as the Plantagenets.
Thomas Becket became Lord Chancellor in 1155.
When in 1162, he resigned to become Archbishop of Canterbury
His friendship with Henry did not survive.

Becket was accused of embezzlement and treason
So he fled abroad for safety as Henry's friendship had now ceased.
On his return Knights murdered him on the altar steps
After Henry's utterance "Will no one rid me of this turbulent priest"?

Dear reader, once again, I ask you to decide
Whether you consider Henry's utterance caused Becket's fate
Or whether it was not meant literally
And was merely spoken when Henry was irate!!

Richard II succeeded Edward III at the age of fourteen
And the council, acting on his behalf, imposed an unpopular poll-tax.
It was intended to apply to rich and poor alike
But was most unfavourable to the poor, according to historical facts.

Wat Tyler had lost control of his followers
And his own death was not altogether clear.
Was he killed attacking the Lord Mayor
Or did a knight's sword end Wat Tyler's career?

Was there ever a person called Robin Hood
With Little John, Maid Marian and his merry band
Who supposedly lived in Sherwood Forest greenwood
Or was it just a legend to warn people of miscreants in the land?

Law breakers, such as highwaymen, smugglers, pick pockets and footpads
Were ready to take advantage and evade the law
So perhaps Robin Hood is merely another legend as a warning to all
And especially as he is supposed to have 'robbed the rich to feed the poor!'

The real history of England as a nation began
After both Saxons and Normans, who had often been beguiled,
Eventually recognised they had interests in common
And, over time, their differences were reconciled.

The banner of St George saw military operations
Far beyond the Alps and Pyrenees
While, at home, our grandest monuments
Were created by degrees.

King John's reign saw the passing
Of the Magna Carta as significant
And the English, in the years that followed,
Established their Empire on the Continent.

The Magna Carta embodied the law
To refuse all kings' permission
To impose taxation without the consent of Parliament.
A necessary provision.

Bubonic plague was brought to our shores
By fleas on rats which came from abroad.
It became known as the Black Death
And a third of the population died, so we record.

After the wars of York and Lancaster
We saw a change in the previous divisions of nobles and the masses.
The constitution of the House of Commons
Assisted the blending of the various classes.

The death of Richard was another historical mystery.
Did he die due to a hunger strike in the castle of Pontefract,
As some historians would have us believe,
Or was Henry IV perhaps involved in a murder pact?

Henry V restarted a war against France
On 25th October 1415 in opposition to our long-term foes.
The battle of Agincourt was successful for the English
Thanks to the arrows fired from their longbows.

In 1429 Joan of Arc left Domremy to visit the Dauphin
And save France, claiming angelic voices gave her the courage.
She was given troops and men's armorial attire
And managed to raise the Orleans' siege.

Joan received no accolades for her achievements.
The French thought her 'angelic voices' were a fake.
The English gave her a supposedly 'fair trial'
And as a 'witch' she was burnt at the stake.

The two princes, Edward and his brother, the Duke of York,
Were imprisoned in the tower
By Richard on the grounds they were illegitimate.
Richard III then assumed monarchical power.

When two young skeletons were found in the seventeenth century
Their death was attributed to Richard.
Yet during his lifetime he never denied he was responsible
And verification after passage of time is most hard!

William Caxton brought the idea of a printing press from Bruges
And there is no doubt there was a need
As handwritten manuscripts were so time consuming
And soon books were readily available to those who could read.

During the period of the Middle Ages
It was decided that no one in future would be above the law
Or would be deprived of its protection
But did this protect the very poor?

Since I wrote the above verses about the princes in the tower
New evidence has come to light
Suggesting Perkin Warbeck could have been Prince Richard
And deserved the throne by right!

3: The Tudor Period

The Middle Ages were years of many phases
With war and hostility never far away
But during the Tudor Dynasty
The English settled for a brighter day.

Henry VII revived the Court of Star Chamber
Which, compared with the local law courts, was an improvement.
It managed to reduce the amount of lawlessness
And rebellions were less evident.

An interesting attempt to obtain monarchical claim
To the throne was by Lambert Simnel, the upstart.
Groomed as the supposed son of the Duke of Clarence
It was doomed to failure from the very start.

The real son at this time was imprisoned in the Tower
So it was easy for the Simnel attempt to be
Thwarted by bringing him out of the Tower
For those in London to see.

But Lambert obtained his moment of fame
And was sent to work in the royal kitchen.
So when you eat Simnel cake in future
Are you not perpetuating his memory, then?

Perkin Warbeck was another pretender to the throne
Claiming he was the younger of the two Princes in the Tower.
The French and Scottish Kings supported his claim
Which ended in his execution in 1499. Not his finest hour!

Henry VIII's desire for England was threefold.
He sought prosperity, peace and markets overseas
And due to his financial expertise
He played his part in achieving these.

Henry VII's son, Arthur, married Catherine of Aragon
At the age of fifteen years, but at sixteen years lost his life.
His younger brother became heir to the English throne
And subsequently King Henry VIII in 1509.
Arthur's widow became his wife.

Had Arthur's young marriage to Catherine ever been consummated?
The church forbade anyone marrying his dead brother's wife
But Henry convinced the Pope who gave his consent
And so began the start of six queens who would share his life.

Henry longed for a male heir to succeed him.
Catherine had not produced a male heir, so Henry a decision
Had to make. If he was to divorce Catherine and marry Anne Boleyn
He first had to nullify the Pope's opposition.

With Parliament's and Archbishop Cranmer's support
He became Head of the Church in England
And this break with the Papacy
Enabled him to wed Anne, as planned.

During the reign of the Tudors
Henry VIII is most remembered, by stealth
Developing the Anglican Church
And plundering the Abbeys to create wealth.

In September 1533 Anne gave birth to a child for Henry.
Unfortunately, it was a daughter, so the King was in despair.
He was tiring of Anne and on a questionable charge of adultery
She was beheaded because Henry still had no male heir!

Jane Seymour produced the heir that Henry wanted
When in October 1537, Edward was born.
Unfortunately, Jane died as a result of the birth.
Henry had but little time to mourn.

Henry next married Anne of Cleves.
Her ugliness earned her the title of the 'Flanders Mare'.
When given recompense for agreeing to the marriage annulment
She readily agreed to end the whole affair.

Catherine Howard was the next of Henry's wives
But she was more flirtatious than Anne Boleyn had ever been.
Perhaps it was inevitable she would suffer the same fate
As she was eventually beheaded on Tower Green.

Henry's final queen was Catherine Parr
Who actually outlived her husband.
She showed great kindness to all his offspring
Or so I understand.

Henry died in 1547 succeeded by his nine-year-old son
Who became Edward VI under Somerset as Lord Protector.
Edward was too young to rule, so Somerset got his way
And as an ardent Protestant his advice was in that sector.

Sir Francis Drake was playing bowls
When, in 1588, the great Armada came.
Once again English strategy won the day
But did Drake really finish his game?

This event most certainly
Established naval supremacy beyond our shores
Setting the whole nation in good stead
For Trafalgar and the two World Wars.

Although Elizabeth I was bodily "a weak and feeble woman"
Her speech at Tilbury was inevitably true.
She had "the heart and stomach of a King
And of a King of England too."

Tobacco was introduced to the English by Sir Walter Raleigh
And since then smoking has caused much loss of life.
It was possibly only slightly less lethal than deaths from smallpox
Or those in battle which, at that time, was still rife.

Elizabeth I from the start of her reign
Was keen to become the people's favourite
Because in the eyes of Catholics and some Protestants
Elizabeth, the daughter of Anne Boleyn, was illegitimate!

Queen Elizabeth died in 1603
Which saw the Tudor Period come to an end
And perhaps the reign of this female monarch
Paved the way for royal male primogeniture to amend.

4: The Stuart Period

On Elizabeth's death James VI of Scotland,
Her cousin Mary's son,
Arrived in England to take the throne
Making Scotland and England union now on.

Everyone remembers the fourth and fifth of November 1605
When Catholic protestors were involved in the gunpowder plot
Which was intended to be detonated as James I
Opened Parliament. Did the plotters succeed? They did not!

Robert Catesby led the Gunpowder plotters.
Guy Fawkes was caught in Parliament's cellars
But did he denounce the other plotters
As many history books often tell us?

Historians sometimes suggest
James I was always in the 'know'
Re the abortive Gunpowder Plot
So perhaps there was no fear of the 'blow'.

The more likely warning given to Parliament
That treachery was afoot re the Gunpowder plot
Is that a conspirator warned a Catholic friend
To attend Parliament on that day he should not!

A search of the cellars was made
And Guy Fawkes was certainly apprehended
But the warning could have been passed on,
Dear reader, how do you think it all ended?

England was ravaged by the Great Plague in 1665
And over one hundred thousand died in London alone, we surmise.
But in 1666 came the Great Fire of London
And perhaps this was a 'blessing in disguise'!

The Great Fire of London spread rapidly
As wooden houses were built too close in those days.
The streets and alleys were also too narrow
For fire appliances to reach the blaze.

The fire started in a baker's shop in Pudding Lane
And created a sentimental sensation
But was not the destruction of overcrowded housing
The opportunity to build more sanitary accommodation?

When the Cavaliers fought the Roundheads in the Civil War
Charles I's fortunes fluctuated with the outcome that he dreaded.
In battles at Edgehill, Marston Moor and Naseby,
Cromwell outsmarted him and he was finally beheaded.

In December 1648 ninety-six Presbyterian members
Were dismissed from Parliament
And the sixty odd members who remained
Became known as the Rump Parliament.

King Charles I was tried by the Rump Parliament
Still maintaining that the authority of the Crown was paramount
And refusing to recognise the court trying him
Alas he was beheaded in January 1649.
The monarch's authority did not count.

Parliament's Roundheads defeated Charles I's Cavaliers
Leaving Oliver Cromwell ruling
Until Charles II assumed monarchical control
And became the next Stuart King.

Oliver and Richard Cromwell both served periods as Lord Protector.
Under Charles II the Church of England was re-established
And Samuel Pepys' diaries recorded the events of the times
Providing historical data when these were published.

Cromwell's army took over as the governing body
Abolishing the House of Lords and establishing the 'Commonwealth'.
Although King Charles II attempted to retake the throne
Cromwell was too strong and Charles escaped to France by stealth.

Cromwell became ruler of the country as Lord Protector
Until his death in 1658 when to his son the title was installed.
A committee of safety dismissed Parliament
And the Long Parliament and Charles II was recalled.

James II ascended the throne in 1685
And his support of the Catholics was well known.
Both his daughters, Mary and Anne, were Protestants
And disapproved of the King's attempt to bar Protestants
from the English throne.

James' second wife was the Catholic Mary of Modena
And she gave birth to a baby son.
There was now a Catholic male heir to the throne
And to avoid this something needed to be done.

Rumours spread that it was not James' baby.
And it had been smuggled into the Queen's bed in a warming pan!
This, however, was not sufficient
to bar Prince James Edward from the throne
So William of Orange was invited over, being of the Protestant clan.

The Glorious Revolution saw William and Mary
Installed as joint sovereigns and in the event
They had to accept a Bill of Rights
Establishing the supremacy of Parliament.

Mary had no children, so James II's daughter Anne
Was elected Queen. Marlborough the French was attacking
Gaining victories at Blenheim, Ramilles, Oudenarde and Malplaquet.
But on his return from the war, favour with the Queen was lacking.

The Bank of England was founded
Which was the start of the National Debt.
The Bank would lend money to the Government at an interest rate
But the capital need never be repaid
provided the interest rate was met.

In 1707 during the later years of Queen Anne's reign
The basis for the United Kingdom of Great Britain was laid
By the Act of Union.
The Scots were to keep their own Church and Law Courts
But share England's Parliament and common rules on trade.

James Edward and Charles Edward, his son,
Known at that time as the Jacobites,
Failed in their attempts to regain the English Throne
Which saw the end of so called 'Stuart Rights'.

A feature of Stuart times were the regular fairs.
Those who drank too much beer would sleep like a baby.
But the 'Press Gang' was always near at hand
And when the drunks awoke they found themselves in the navy.

In 1679 legal rights for everyone was Shaftesbury's legacy
When the Habeas Corpus Act was passed, one might say.
This made it law that anyone arrested
Should be brought before the courts without delay.

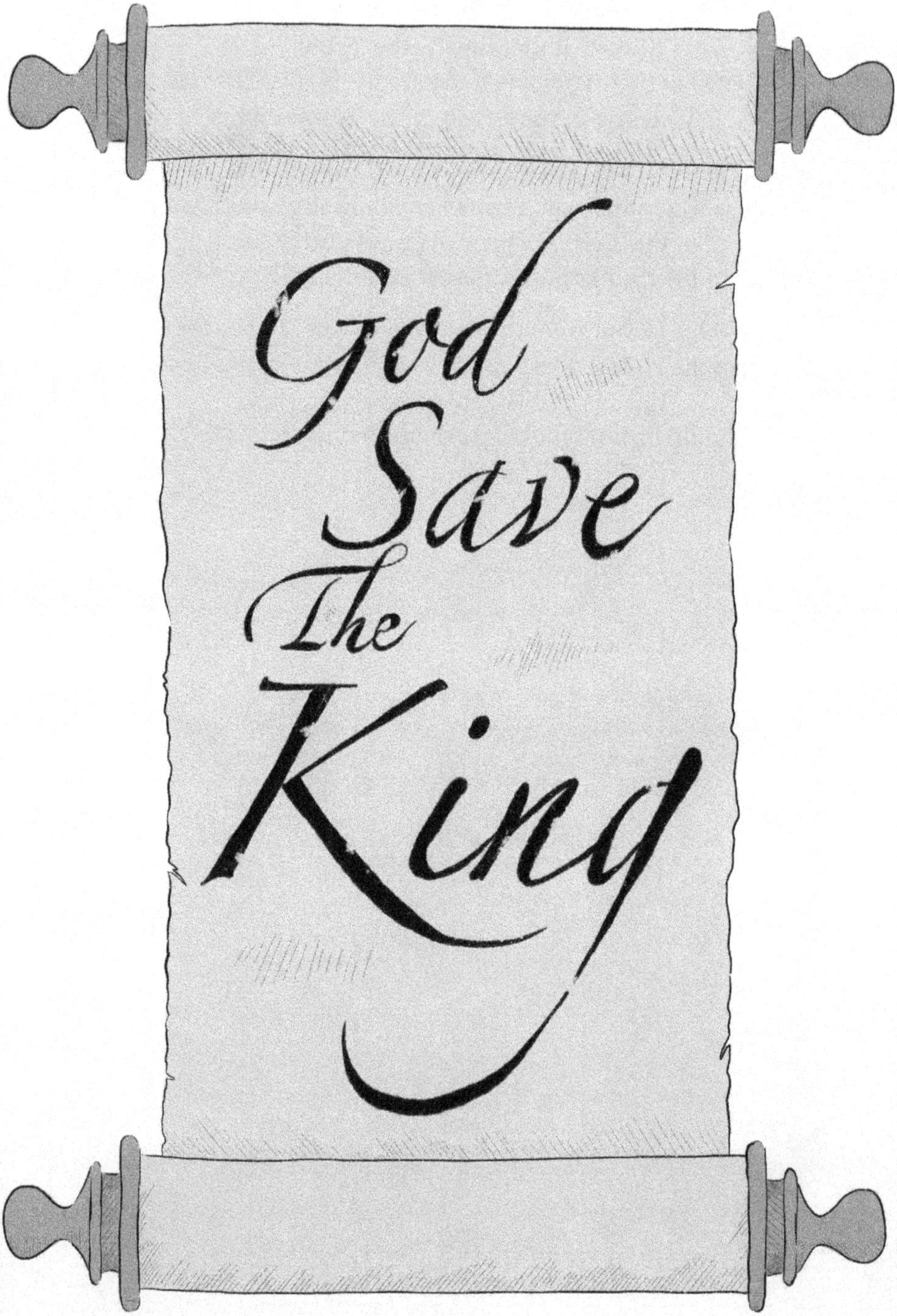
God
Save
The
King

5: The Georgian Era

When Anne died in 1714 without surviving heirs,
Her German cousin George became the King of the English nation
And as the Jacobite Rebellions of 1715 and '45 both failed
We finally achieved a Protestant restoration.

Due to George I's reluctance to learn the English language
His meetings with ministers was obviously a problem.
A prominent minister was needed to become the 'first among equals'
Who would be known in future as the PM.

By 1721 the office of Prime Minister had emerged
And Robert Walpole was destined to be the first.
The South Sea Company took over thirty million pounds of National Debt
But it was not long before the 'South Sea Bubble' burst.

During the war between France and Britain in the 1740s in India
Dupleix saw an opportunity to defeat the British.
Clive, captain of the military wing of the East India Company,
Led the attack and Dupleix did not get his wish.

Siraj-ud-Daulah seized Calcutta, a British Trading Post,
And crammed 146 prisoners into a guardroom.
Only 23 survived and Clive defeated Daulah at Plassey in 1757.
The 'Black Hole' of Calcutta was another case of doom.

George II is remembered for being the last English monarch
To actually into battle lead his men.
It had taken many centuries for this practice to end
And occurred in 1743 at the Battle of Dettingen.

Drury Lane actors introduced a song entitled 'God Save the King'
As they feared the worst after victory at Prestonpans by Charles Edward.
The song was also sung in other London theatres
And its adoption as our National Anthem was assured.

George II's grandson succeeded to the throne as George III
And during his reign Wellington achieved familiarity
At Waterloo aided by Blucher and the Prussians
Together with Napoleon's disability.

George III was a much-respected King of England
But some historians record him for unfortunate events.
Was our loss of the American colonies due to George alone
Or should we be looking for other miscreants?

George III reigned for sixty years, a record at the time.
Only later was this exceeded by two English Queens.
Both Victoria and Elizabeth II broke George's record
But let us remember George III whichever way history leans.

Why do historians often dwell to excess regarding George III 's madness'
Producing a distorted account which caused considerable hysteria?
Actually, he proved to be an active and successful politician
And later medical evidence suggests he suffered from porphyria.

King George III assisted Sunday Schools and prison reform.
His knowledge of botany enabled him to indulge in agricultural activity.
He wrote pamphlets under the name of Ralph Robinson
And supporting the General Board of Agriculture he improved productivity

The Stamp Act of 1765 was an attempt to tax the thirteen American Colonies.
However, as the Colonists were not represented in the English Parliament
The cry was 'No Taxation without Representation'
And this became the slogan for all duties the Colonists resent.

The British East India Company's monopoly on tea trade to North America
Meant an exemption from import duties which the Colonists abhor
But did this really result in four hundred cases of tea
Being ceremoniously dumped into Boston Harbour?

On 4th July 1776 the American Colonists declared their independence
And George III never recovered from the colonial loss,
But did it contribute to his future 'madness'
Or simply make him permanently cross?

In 1787 William Wilberforce, MP for Hull,
Set out 'slavery laws' to amend
After Bills in the Commons were at first rejected
The abolitionists in 1807 successfully brought slavery in England to an end.

Although British ships no longer carried slaves
And British traders could no longer make a profit from this trade,

Slavery still existed in various parts of the British Empire
Until, William IV in 1833, an Act finally ended this long tirade.

On 1st January 1801 the union of Great Britain and Ireland took place.
St Patrick's flag was added to those of St George and St Andrew, it appears.
Irish members were admitted to the House of Commons
And the House of Lords became available to Irish Peers.

British trade was affected during the Napoleonic Wars.
It was the poor who suffered most, as is usually the case,
As a series of bad harvests caused prices to rise
And wages remained low for the working populace.

During the Napoleonic wars
A French invasion was feared the most,
So Martello Towers, copied from the French,
Were constructed to defend the southern coast.

Was the expense of £3,000 for each Martello Tower
Really a necessary expense and who was to blame?
John Moore had experienced their effectiveness as French forts
But in England they were never tested as the invasion never came.

Emperor Napoleon attempted to invade England.
He realised he needed control of the channel so to do.
But Nelson declined to attack in line ahead
And decided to break the enemy line in two.

The victory at Trafalgar was marred when Nelson was shot
By a sniper in the rigging of the French ship Redoutable.
This was a massive blow to English naval supremacy
And its effect on naval history was unaccountable.

It was at the Battle of Waterloo that the Duke of Wellington
Over Napoleon gained his impressive victory.
But without Prussian help would this have been the case
And would it have changed the course of history?

Sir Robert Peel introduced the police force in 1829
One shilling or a 'bob' was the daily pay deal.
Is that why we call present policeman 'bobbies'
Or does it originate from the Christian name of Peel?

6: The Industrial and Agrarian Revolutions

The eighteenth century saw the start of the Industrial Revolution
England being the pioneers in textile industry.
John Kay, James Hargreaves and Richard Arkwright
All played their parts in the growth of the textile factory.

You would be right to assume such progress had its price
And in the nineteenth century the Factory Acts, so they say,
Were to safeguard women and children working there
But were workers attracted when Arkwright offered the paid holiday?

England's industrial revolution is epitomised in the phrase
'Necessity is the mother of invention'.
My old history teacher taught me this
And my memory allows its retention.

In 1733 John Kay invented the Flying Shuttle
For speeding up the weaving process, so it seems.
Later he devised a faster spinning wheel
But fearing the loss of jobs the workers smashed up his machines.

When James Hargreaves' Spinning Jenny, named after his wife,
Was succeeded by Richard Arkwright's Spinning Frame
producing stronger thread,
It could not be worked by hand. It needed at first horsepower
And later a water wheel so factories replaced spinning in the homestead.

Telford and MacAdam were responsible for road building
And Turnpike trusts meant travellers had to pay tolls.
Admittedly vehicles were not as heavy or as numerous as today
But the well-built roads were devoid of today's potholes.

In addition to developments in the manufacture of cotton
England also took the lead with steam, steel and coal.
For the transport of bulky goods the railways were needed
And in 1825 the Stockton and Darlington line provided that goal.

Further development came with James Watt's Steam Engine in 1775
Which allowed railways to develop as a form of transport
And Henry Cort's purification of iron in 1783 enabled factories to be created,
Railway tracks to be built and machinists to be sought.

In 1830 the Liverpool to Manchester Railway
meant railways had come to stay
When railways carried passengers as well as freight
And Bradshaw's railway timetables, still marvelled at today,
Avoided trains being missed because travellers arrived too late.

Iron was needed for the increased demand for machinery
The Darbys used coke instead of charcoal for smelting iron
To avoid the iron being contaminated by impurities.
In 1777 Abraham Darby crossed the River Severn
with a bridge of cast iron.

Steamships took people and goods across the sea.
Steam trains carried goods and commuters quicker than before
And with the development of relatively cheap fares
It opened up seaside holidays for the very poor.

Josiah Wedgwood's mass production of porcelain
Required safe and cheaper conveyance for his wares.
He, therefore, whole heartedly supported canals
An' gladly became one of the prime investors.

Francis Egerton, third Duke of Bridgewater,
was responsible for canal development.
To aid him in this he needed an engineer to construct
His first canal from Manchester to Worsley to transport coal.
He chose James Brindley who crossed
the River Irwell with an aqueduct.

Enclosure of this land allowed for sheep and cattle grazing
As well as the four-stage rotation of crops Britain adopts.
Lord Townshend became known as 'Turnip Townshend'.
His four-year rotation included turnips or other root crops.

Apart from Townshend's use of turnips
In other years the land would be seeded
With the growth of cereal crops
Followed by peas, beans or clover without fallow being needed.

Large landowners, under enclosure, were the gainers
As they could afford the ensuing cost
Whereas the poorer tenant farmers had to farm less productive land
And as the common land had been removed, again they lost.

Voting at elections prior to 1832
Was restricted to sinecurists
Of the rotten and pocket boroughs.
It was time to enfranchise the upper middle class and industrialists.

Several more Acts were needed before
The right to vote was eventually won
By all men and women in England
Provided they were at least twenty-one.

Enfranchisement had been achieved
For those classed as adults in 1928
But it took a further 41 years
To allow eighteen-year-olds to participate.

In 1834 six farm-labourers of Tolpuddle
Formed a union and an oath was versed
Which in those days was illegal.
Two years later their 'transportation punishment' was reversed.

7: The Victorian Age

In 1837 Victoria became Queen at the age of eighteen.
Her beloved husband, Prince Albert, died in 1861.
She remained our Queen until 1901
But was never the same after Albert had gone.

Her mourning lasted for the rest of her life
With her devoted man-servant John Brown.
On occasions she appeared in public
She wore the black widow's bonnet but not her crown.

It was useful for Queen Victoria to know
The population distribution from the census count.
But was it not also used to determine taxation?
Both who should pay and what amount?

The Chartists formed a People's Charter
Demanding universal male suffrage and MP's pay
Causing riots in 1839 and 1842. But in the passage of time
These and other demands eventually saw the light of day.

In 1840 Rowland Hill introduced the Penny Black
Which was the very first postage stamp to appear.
But was this regarded as universal penny post
As the roads were poorly maintained for many a year?

In 1842 a law was passed forbidding
Children under 10 working in mines and women too.
No longer would children be operating trap doors
To let the trucks and barrows through.

The Corn Laws were designed to keep landlords solvent
By imposing a duty on imported grain.
This inevitably kept food prices high
Which meant that the poor workers lost again.

Repeal of the Corn Laws came in 1846
Thanks to the efforts of Cobden and Bright
But sadly it came too late for Ireland
As the Irish potato famine was at its height.

In 1851 Britain's industrial supremacy was complete
But Victoria needed the world to become aware of such a case.
Her husband, Prince Albert, by supporting the Great Exhibition
Ensured the success of the Crystal Palace.

Five hundred deaths in just five days in London in 1854
Were due to cholera. Doctor John Snow felt this slaughter
From a disease which was rife and no one knew the cause.
He discovered that the source of cholera was contaminated water.

Queen Victoria survived several assassination attempts.
No wonder history indicates that she was not amused.
However, there is no evidence that she ever said "We are not amused".
Do you believe these words, by the Queen, were ever used?

Florence Nightingale, the most memorable of nurses,
Was appalled how the injured were cared for
And the 'Lady with the Lamp' went beyond her call of duty
When caring for soldiers injured in the Crimean War.

In 1865 David Livingstone went on his second visit to Africa.
Five years passed and a move was made to find him, we assume.
Henry Morton Stanley eventually met him at Ujiji
Supposedly with the words "Doctor Livingstone, I presume?"

The population of Victorian London grew at an alarming rate
And the transportation system found it could not cope.
So, in spite of opposition, Charles Pearson's dream came true
With the London Underground giving commuters new hope.

But history is not just about monarchy
And many changes took place during Victoria's reign.
In 1891 free education was introduced
But parents' loss defeated children's gain.

Child labour was accepted as a necessity
Even after 1842 when employment of children under ten
in mines was withdrawn.
Other work was expected from their offspring
To swell the families' low incomes
almost from the day they were born.

Victorian child labour was an integral part of family life
And for most children normal childhood was forbidden.
The boys were employed in sweeping chimneys from the inside
And making nails while the girls were making ribbon.

Can we always be sure whether events are true or false
Because some historical stories may sound rather odd.
Please, dear reader, make up your own mind.
Was there ever a barber called Sweeney Todd?

Books written in Victorian times included horrific villains
Count Dracula and Frankenstein's Monster have never been forgotten.
But did they compare with the real villains of the age
Namely Jack the Ripper and Mary Ann Cotton?

Jack the Ripper killed eight women but was never caught.
Mary Ann Cotton poisoned four husbands
and many children but by artfulness
Managed to avoid suspicion over a period of years
By changing her name between marriages and frequently her address.

Queen Victoria died in January 1901
And a brief funeral service was held at Windsor
Before her committal to be laid to rest in the mausoleum
In Windsor Home Park where Albert had been interred
many years before.

On Victoria's death the throne passed to her son, Edward VII,
An 'irresponsible playboy' was his late mother's experience,
But on becoming King he settled down
And achieved cordial relations with neighbouring France.

8: Early 20th Century

In the early twentieth century the internal combustion engine
pre-empted the car
Although in England development was cut short.
This was because a pedestrian with a red flag
Had to precede all mechanically propelled transport.

A further hindrance to real progress
Even though the repeal of the red flag had been passed,
Was a speed limit of twelve miles per hour
Which in the early twentieth century was quite fast.

Edward VII made his first motor car journey in 1899
But it was in a Daimler not an English car
Because Germany, France and the United States
Had a lead on British car manufacture.

When Charles Stewart Rolls met Henry Royce
Manufacture began to look up in the motor industry
And I don't have to tell you their contribution
For their names are known worldwide in history.

Road transport at best was a bumpy ride
Until inventions assisted both comfort and speed.
Inflated tyres replaced solid rubber
And double-decker motor buses supplied another need.

Another important milestone in the history of transport
Was air travel which developed so soon
After Louis Bleriot crossed the English Channel by air
And air transport no longer relied on the hot-air balloon.

Communication by voice over long distance
Came in 1876 with the telephone by Alexander Graham Bell
And along with Guglielmo Marconi
Wireless transmission by radio waves was invented as well.

The Liberals came to power in 1906
With David Lloyd George elected from the working class
And Winston Churchill, who started as a Conservative MP,
Joined the Liberals and Labour exchanges came to pass.

The Chancellor of the Exchequer was David Lloyd George
And in 1908 he introduced old-age pensions.
The following year in the 'People's Budget'
Taxes were raised to offset possible German intentions.

In May 1910 Edward VII died
The throne passed to George V, Edward's second son,
The elder brother having died
But Lloyd George's laws were carried on.

National Health insurance was introduced
By which he hoped to improve the nation's medical aid
And to satisfy the Chartists
Salaries to MP's would be paid.

Kier Hardy set out to form an independent Labour Party
And in 1911 James Ramsay MacDonald became the leader.
Initially they had forty–two elected members after the 1910 election
But they needed financial support and trade unions were the main 'feeder'.

In 1912 the Titanic set out on her maiden voyage
And publicity of the day described it as unsinkable.
But the Titanic struck an iceberg
And a tragedy occurred which everyone believed unthinkable.

In 1903 Emmeline Pankhurst sought to work for female suffrage
When the Women's Social and Political Union was established.
The government were not prepared to discuss the matter
So Mrs Pankhurst did not immediately achieve what she had wished.

The suffragettes then resorted to 'nuisance tactics'
Chaining themselves to railings, fire raising
and heckling Government spokesmen,
By the 'Cat and Mouse Act' when imprisoned
they went on hunger strikes
Only to be released but on recuperation to be returned to prison again.

In 1913 at the Derby, Emily Davison committed suicide
By throwing herself under the King's horse.
This tragedy aroused sympathy for the Suffragette
And votes for women were considered in due course.

It was 1918 when the vote was received by women over thirty years
But to have equality with men in voting rights
They had to wait another ten long years.
So the Suffragettes at last had won their fights.

Undoubtedly the part played by women in the First World War
Was responsible for them highlighting their talents
And being treated as equals to the men folk in many fields.
However, genuine equality will only be achieved
when financial rewards are in balance.

9: Two World Wars and an Abdication

After Archduke Franz Ferdinand of Austria
Was assassinated along with his wife,
Britain became involved in World War One.
But to be over by Christmas? .. not on your life!

Zeppelins were launched on England by the Germans
At the start of the First World War.
It was a new wave of invaders, this time from the air,
Which our mastery of the sea had repelled before.

Zeppelins, however, were unreliable
and were soon replaced by Gotha aircraft
Which could carry a greater bombing load.
But it was to British anti-aircraft defences and brave fighter pilots
That our airspace defence was owed.

British casualties were very heavy in the first years of the war.
The British fought from trenches but little ground was won
At Ypres, on the Somme and Passchendaele
Showing the failure of trench warfare as a strategy in World War One.

The allies had to withstand poison gas attacks.
In 1917 tanks replaced the earliest forms of war weapons pulled by horses.
Over six million women worked in industry or the services
And a similar number of men served in the forces.

George V detested the First World War
And was loyal to common humanity
Advocating humane treatment for German prisoners
And striving for national unity.

Churchill had many successes but as First Lord of the Admiralty
His attack on the Dardanelles proved to be a doomed campaign,
Expecting the navy to gain victory initially without troop back-up.
When troops were finally sent, it proved in vain.

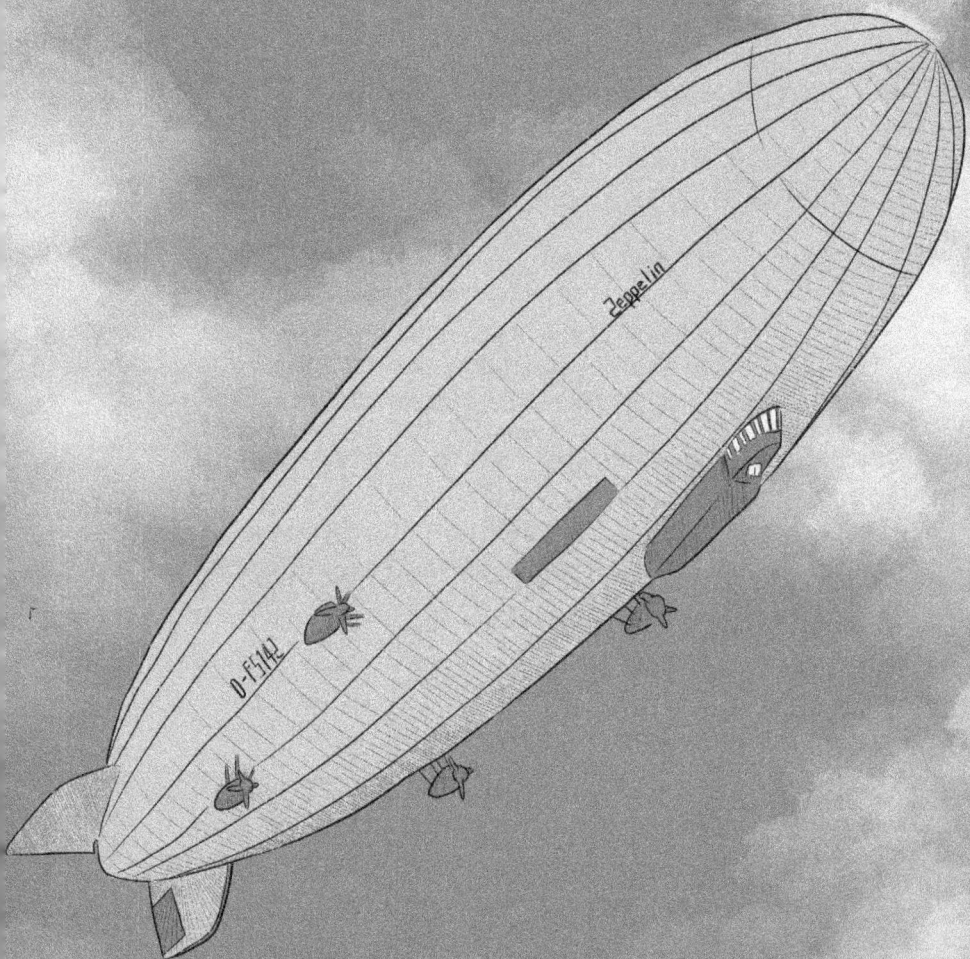

Britain's food and raw materials were brought by sea.
Churchill organised English battle cruisers to destroy German cruisers
And at Jutland in 1916, although Britain sustained heavy losses,
The German fleet were no longer a threat so they were the losers.

On 17th July 1917 England was ruled by King George V
And the pressure during the war years against the German nation
Made the Royal Family name of Saxe-Coburg-Gotha most inappropriate
So replacing it with the House of Windsor was accepted with elation.

George V grew in popularity as his reign progressed.
He believed changes were needed if the monarchy was to last.
This included communication with the English populace
So he introduced to the airwaves a Christmas radio broadcast

This practice was continued by future Kings and Queens
And the monarch's Christmas broadcast is still carried out today
Allowing the Royal Family to come closer to the nation
And its importance in this regard surely means that it will stay.

The Flying Scotsman is the most famous steam locomotive in the world.
It was built in Doncaster and displayed
at the British Empire Exhibition in 1924.
It began the first ever regular non-stop service from London to Edinburgh
And it achieved its record-breaking 100 miles per hour run in 1934.

1926 was the 'annus mirabilis' for the House of Windsor
As on 21st April Elizabeth Alexandra Mary was born
And on 19th October Lionel Logue met George VI
And the latter's lifetime stammer would soon be gone.

On 4th May 1926 England was involved in a General Strike
Hoping to achieve shorter working hours and an increase in pay.
The miners' unions' slogan was 'Not a penny off the wage,
Not a minute on the day'.

We know King George V and Prince Edward
Never came together as father and 'kid'.
Edward never accepted that an individual needed homage
And failed to realise that the institution of monarchy did.

On his brief accession on George V's death
You can decide, dear reader, if this was really true
That Edward had the clocks retimed from being half an hour fast!
But we do know for certain he was the first reigning monarch who flew.

Edward's abdication was known by all who lived through it
But do you realise how hard was his choice?
The conflict between private happiness and public duty
Was not only coming from his voice.

A morganatic solution was suggested
Whereby Mrs Simpson would not be Queen but King's Consort
But this was unacceptable to Edward
Who refused to give it a second thought.

Some hoped he'd be crowned and that passage of time
Might somehow provide a solution.
Edward refused to be crowned, concealing a lie,
Which would inevitably lead to confusion.

Edward believed everyone should be allowed to marry
Whom they chose, provided the marriage was legal,
As he was truly in love with Mrs Simpson
He felt it should apply were you a commoner or regal.

The First World War lost so many killed or permanently wounded
It was thought it would be the last war to be fought
But in 1939 hostilities were again resumed
And another World War victory was sought.

Germans were left smarting from the Versailles Treaty
Which ended the First World War.
They felt they were harshly treated and blamed for the whole affair
So Hitler looked for scapegoats and the Jews came to the fore.

Hitler's secret police segregated Jews
And the depletion of all of Jewish birth became his ambition.
With the introduction of concentration camps
German Jews had no choice but submission.

The Royal Air Force was formed in April 1918
And it undoubtedly came to our aid
When the Luftwaffe, bombing in the Second World War,
Tried unsuccessfully to invade.

Neville Chamberlain met Adolf Hitler in 1938.
To avert pending war would be sublime.
But appeasement did not halt the German aggression
And there was 'no peace with honour' or 'peace in our time'.

Even before the War started
Foster homes were sought for evacuation
Of children who lived in large cities
To the countryside. It often widened their education.

But as with all innovations
There was good and bad foster care
And for some children it was a positive step.
Others regarded evacuation with despair.

On 3rd September 1939 we entered the Second World War
When Hitler invaded Poland whom we had promised to defend.
We were not really prepared for defeating Germany
But thanks to brave conscripts we achieved a successful end.

A new Prime Minister was certainly needed
At the outset of another World War
And when Churchill took over this important role
George VI realised his worth, that's for sure.

To add to the latter and convince the nation
That he was a reliable defender,
He used four words to raise people's hopes,
Namely "We shall never surrender".

Churchill had re-joined the Conservatives and was Chancellor.
A good choice for the nation, as it proved,
When he became Prime Minister of the Coalition Government in 1940
As his guidance saved the country which he loved.

When Winston Churchill became PM at the outset of World War Two
We badly needed a bold innovator
And apart from someone capable of achieving victory
The country also needed an experienced orator.

He kept the nation's spirits up and gave them belief
By numerous heartwarming speeches:
"We will fight them in the fields, in the streets, in the hills,
On the landing grounds and on the beaches."

The death of George V and the abdication of Edward VIII
Meant George VI was now in line for the throne
But as he had not been prepared for this unexpected event
He had less than one month to atone.

Although George VI was shy by nature
He relied heavily on his wife, Queen Elizabeth, for support
And nowhere was this more evident
In the years the Second World War brought.

Britain had no alternative but to declare war on Germany
When the Nazi invasion of Poland had taken place
But did Hitler seriously think
Britain would ally with the German race?

Churchill became Prime Minister as a replacement for Chamberlain
National unity by coalition was his target to get.
In a speech in the House of Commons he proclaimed
There would be "Blood, toil, tears and sweat."

Hitler planned an invasion of south-eastern England
Relying on air and torpedo attack to cripple our fleet.
But with the help of radar's advance warnings
British pilots refused to accept defeat.

Fighter Command was praised by Churchill
And to the pilots of Spitfires and Hurricanes it was due.
"Never before in the field of human conflict
Was so much owed by so many to so few".

To eke out our food supplies for the population
Those in England were content
To encourage families to grow their own food.
Hence the increased demand for an allotment.

London and England's cities and ports
Withstood the Luftwaffe's eight weeks aerial onslaught,
Known to historians as The Blitz,
But the English defence cut their attacks short.

In early 1940 merchant shipping bringing food
Was sunk by German submarines so rationing was needed
And to withstand nightly bombing raids
Government guidelines had to be conscientiously heeded.

With food supplies from abroad uncertain
Rationing was introduced to keep hunger at bay
But was everyone treated fairly
When 'spivs' catered for those who could pay?

Hitler hoped to halt Britain's shipping lanes
To stop food and other goods arriving at ports.
France's fall in 1940 gave German U-boats free access
Until America joined the war with its cohorts.

Thanks to the failure by the German Luftwaffe
To establish superiority in the air
'Operation Sea Lion' by the Germans
Was more than the supposed invaders ever dare.

The British Expeditionary Force evacuated Dunkirk
With the help of countless small boats in the month of May.
This was a bad start for the allies against Hitler's might
But it at least allowed the British to fight another day.

At Dunkirk nearly 400,000 men were evacuated
Thanks to the bravery of those who manned the boats which they were in.
But let us not forget those left dead on French beaches
And the loss sustained back home by their next of kin.

The Tripartite Pact of September 1940
allied Germany with Italy and Japan
But Churchill's appreciation of the Spitfire and Hurricane pilots
was very true.
Together with American troops and supplies reaching Britain
It was obvious the allies were already 'turning the screw'.

With France defeated and before America entered the War
Britain appeared to be the last barrier for Germany's might.
But we must not forget we had hidden resources
As our Commonwealth brotherhood joined in the fight.

Pearl Harbour saw the sinking of American ships
When Germany's ally, the Japanese, made a mistake.
Would America otherwise have come to England's aid?
To the allies it was merely the 'icing on the cake'.

Barnes Wallace's perfection of the revolutionary bouncing bomb
Enabled England to destroy the dams of Mohne, Surpe and Eder.
Operation Chastise was the name of this significant onslaught
Led by Guy Gibson, RAF's 617 Squadron Leader.

When the allies stormed the beaches of Normandy
On the sixth of June 1944,
A foothold in Western Europe was established
And D-Day, as it is known, ultimately ended the war.

Within a few days 326,000 troops and 50,000 vehicles
And 100,000 tons of war materials were landed
on the Normandy beachhead
Of Omaha, Utah, Sword, Juno and Gold.
The cost, however, was over 10,000 casualties
with approximately 4,000 dead.

D-Day took meticulous planning and execution
If the objective of freedom was to be solved
But we must never forget the selfless bravery
Of all the allies involved.

Churchill was right to be cautious
Knowing D-Day was only the beginning.
Liberation of France was still to be achieved
The battle of Normandy needed winning.

Opposing Field Marshalls, Rommel and Montgomery,
Led their respective forces' armed attack
And in spite of heavy losses
The allies knew there was no turning back.

Perhaps the celebrations on the sixth of June
Were a little premature!
In retrospect it is easy to think so.
Should we not have waited until total victory was sure?

On the eighth of May 1945 war with Germany ceased
And celebrations for VE day were universal so
Winston Churchill added a note of caution
As Japan was still a formidable foe.

The future Queen, Princess Elizabeth, and her sister, Margaret
Mingled with the crowd and enjoyed the celebration.
Elizabeth was dressed in her ATS uniform
Showing her commitment to the wartime needs of our nation.

The Second World War was the deadliest conflict in history
Killing more than fifty-five million military personnel and civilians.
Apart from the death toll did not the number of casualties
Also inevitably run into millions?

However, we must not forget those who died in the War
And not everyone who had lost someone could participate in a celebration.
We will not forget the fallen when Remembrance Day comes around
For the British Legion's support in this is as good as any nation.

Although victory in Europe was secured on 8th May 1945
The Japanese were still a threat to peace
Until August when atomic bombs on Hiroshima and Nagasaki
Hastened the sought-for armistice.

During 1944 a famous battle was fought in the Netherlands
And this history would not be complete without giving it a mention.
It was known as Operation Market Garden
And had it been successful the War could have ended,
which was the intention.

'Market' referred to the ground offensive
once troops had been parachuted in
And 'Garden' to the capture of the Rhine's key bridges
leading to Arnhem.
However, the parachutists landed some way from their target
And the Germans in the Nazi-occupied Netherlands
were able to capture them.

The troops involved British, American and Polish forces
And of the British 1,600 were killed and 6,500 were captured.
It was one of the largest airborne assaults in history
And of those who took part their heroism was assured.

10: The Second Elizabethan Age

In April 1926 Elizabeth Alexandra Mary Windsor was born.
Whatever she regarded in her early years as a personal ambition
Was drastically changed after Edward abdicated
and father George became King
Because now Elizabeth found herself next in the line of succession.

Throughout the war years the Royal Family stayed together
So Elizabeth and her sister Margaret did not seek safety by leaving the city.
This obviously created much respect from the English people
And by visiting areas hit by bombs, George gained in popularity.

Elizabeth married Prince Philip in 1947 and on the death of George VI
In 1952 she was proclaimed the Queen at the age of twenty-five.
In 1961 her visit to Ghana was advised against but her determination
Indicated a dedication to the Commonwealth
which Elizabeth insisted must survive.

Queen Elizabeth's coronation took place in 1953
And this year was undoubtedly one of the best.
Not only did we welcome a new monarch to the throne
But Edmund Hillary and Sherpa Tenzing conquered Everest.

Britain led the world in the peaceful use of atomic energy
And Queen Elizabeth showed her support to one and all
By officiating in the autumn of 1956
At the opening of the first nuclear power station at Calder Hall.

In 1970 the Open University opened its doors
To anyone desirous of furthering their education
At home, without the necessity of attending a university.
Radio and television played their part in programming for the nation.

Taxation changed from purchase tax to VAT
When our coinage succumbed to decimalisation,
A necessary change as a forerunner to electronic computers
But was not universally welcomed by an aged population.

1972 saw the Silver Wedding of Elizabeth and Philip.
Festivities were held as you will understand.
Five years later a Silver Jubilee was achieved by the Queen
Which saw beacon bonfires lit across the land.

After decades of enmity between England and France
The joint Anglo-French project of the world's first super-service aeroplane
Became airborne in 1977 in the name of Concorde,
But the cost to both countries was a severe financial strain.

The Queen's eldest son Prince Charles and heir apparent
In 1981 married Lady Diana Spencer as a successor to the throne was due.
Unfortunately, the marriage was rather crowded, as Diana said
And resulted in divorce in 1992.

Margaret Thatcher became Prime Minister in 1979
And was the very first female to hold the post.
She managed to reduce the amount of Britain's contribution
To the EEC, possibly the achievement she valued the most.

In 1982 Argentina claimed sovereignty over the Falkland Islands
And PM Margaret Thatcher took appropriate action.
The Falklands were reclaimed by England
And since there has been no positive reaction.

The prompt action in defending the Falklands
From aggression by Argentinian invasion
Enabled Britain to maintain the islands' independence.
Another victory for the English Nation.

In October 1984 a bomb exploded in the Royal Hotel
In Brighton at the Conservative Party Conference.
Margaret Thatcher narrowly escaped death
And the shock throughout the nation was immense.

It is not surprising that the Queen regarded 1992 as an 'annus horribilis'.
Prince Andrew separated from Sarah, Princess Anne got a divorce,
Prince Charles separated from Diana
and finally there was a fire at Windsor Castle.
It is difficult to imagine that the year could have been worse.

Charles and Diana divorced in 1996 and in the following year
In a car crash in Paris, Diana was killed.
In 1999 Prince Edward married Sophie Rhys-Jones,
A much-needed love story, or so it was billed.

2022 saw the Platinum Jubilee of Queen Elizabeth II,
She was Britain's longest reigning monarch and sage.
Queen Victoria had previously held that record.
Elizabeth's death in 2022 saw the end of the second Elizabethan Age.

With her husband Prince Phillip, in the King George VI Memorial Chapel
On 19th September 2022 Queen Elizabeth II was laid to rest.
Of all the British monarchs who had gone before
She undoubtedly proved to be the best.

Her entire life was spent in serving the people
Of Britain and the Commonwealth of Nations
And as head of the Armed Forces
She played a vital and sincere role at all State occasions.

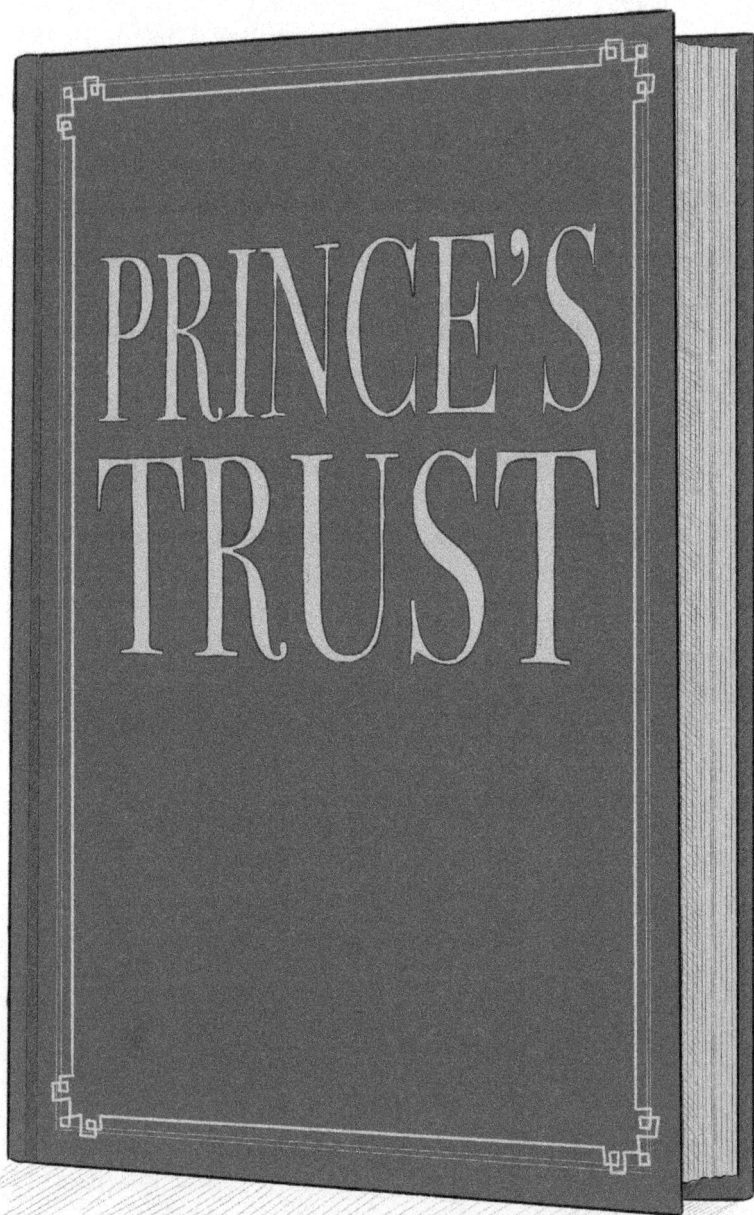

PRINCE'S TRUST

11: Charles III and Heirs to the English Throne

Prince Charles was invested as Prince of Wales at Caernarfon Castle.
He made his maiden speech in the House of Lords in 1974.
The first royal to do so since Edward VII
Almost 100 years before.

Charles needed heirs to succeed him on the throne
And on 29th July 1981 he chose the girl he would marry
In Diana Spencer. The marriage did not last
But provided Charles with two sons, namely William and Harry.

Inevitably divorce came on the 28th August 1996
And Charles resumed his courtship with Camilla Parker Bowles.
After a period for the country to appreciate the possible outcome
Their obvious happiness would help both to develop their respective roles.

On 9th April 2005 when Prince Charles married Camilla
It was with the consent of the Queen, the Church and the Government.
Charles could now prepare himself for his life as King
And Camilla would become his trusty confidante.

On 8th September 2022 Prince Charles ascended to the British throne.
He was the nation's longest-serving heir apparent
And he immediately promised his lifelong service
to the nation and Commonwealth.
Although to assume control after Queen Elizabeth's reign
will not be easy in any event.

The years ahead with their social, economic and international problems
Will not be easy for a seventy-four-year-old King.
But let us hope his health allows him to carry out his royal duties
As I am sure his mother would have been hoping.

Queen Elizabeth announced on the eve of her seventieth year as Queen
That on Charles' succession Camilla would become
Queen Consort as Charles fervently wanted.
In 2018 leaders of the Commonwealth agreed
That Prince Charles should succeed Queen Elizabeth
as the next Commonwealth Head.

His most important contribution to society has been the Prince's Trust,
The charity he founded to assist vulnerable youth make their dreams reality.
It has proved one of the most successful funding charities
And more than a million youths have benefitted in totality.

The succession after King Charles III is already in good hands
With Prince William as the rightful heir
Followed in due course by Prince George.
So the monarch's popularity looks promising for many a year.

We know not what life in future years will be like.
Let us hope it will be good for all nations.
But with the advent of virtual reality and Artificial Intelligence,
In an unsettled world, it will severely test future generations.

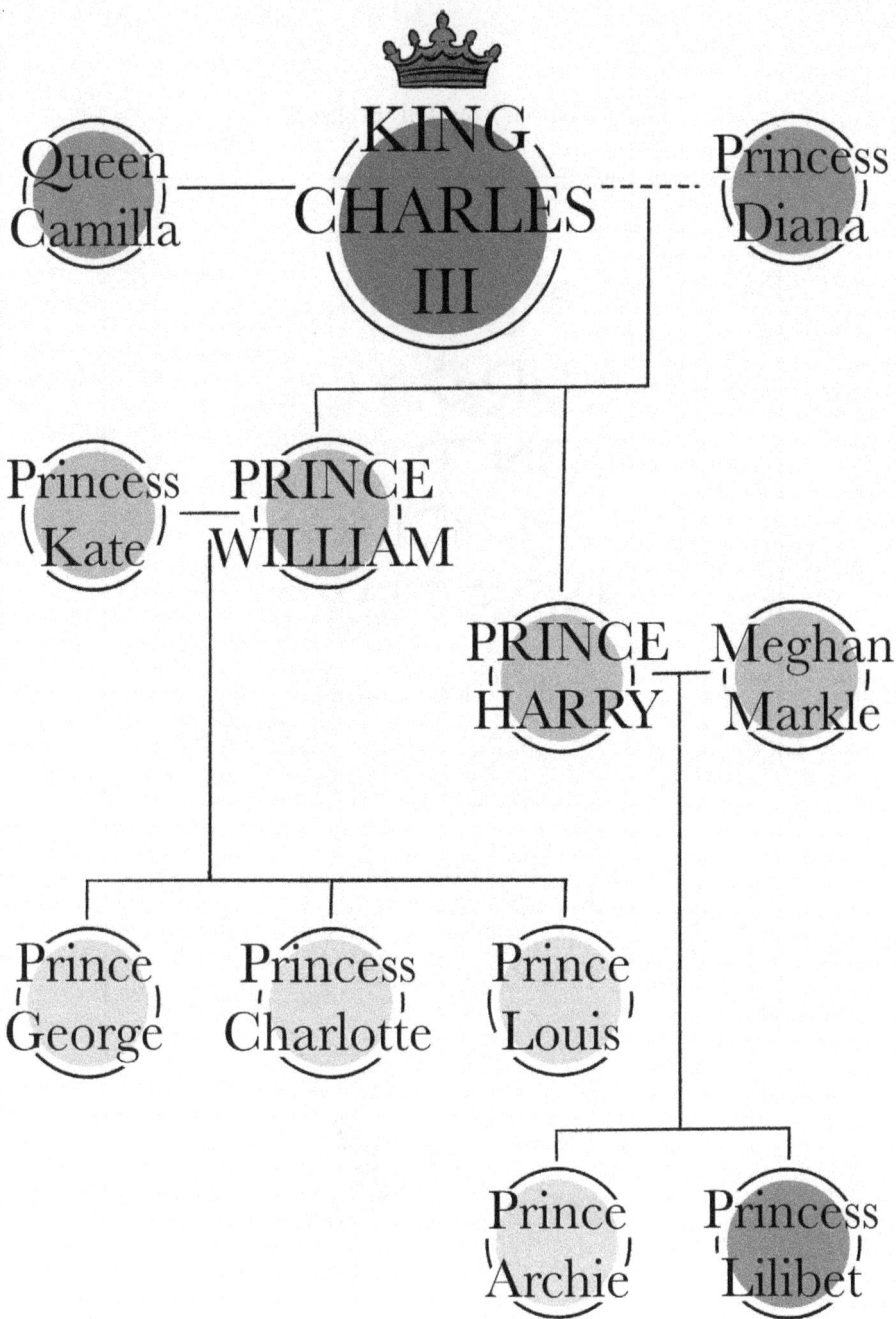

King Charles III
Queen Camilla
Princess Diana
Princess Kate — Prince William
Prince Harry — Meghan Markle
Prince George
Princess Charlotte
Prince Louis
Prince Archie
Princess Lilibet

ARE YOU **SURE** YOU **DON T** LIKE READING **POETRY?**

John William Skepper